Get yourself promoted

How to move up the career ladder

A & C Black • London

0713 675195 3813 84

© A & C Black Publishers Ltd 2006

First published in 2006 by
A & C Black Publishers Ltd
38 Soho Square
London W1D 3HB

British Library Cataloguing in Publication Data
A CIP record for this book is available from the British Library.

ISBN-10: 0–7136–7519–5
ISBN-13: 978–0–7136–7519–1

Design by Fiona Pike, Pike Design, Winchester
Typeset by RefineCatch Limited, Bungay, Suffolk
Printed in Italy by Legoprint

A & C Black uses paper produced with elemental chlorine-free pulp, harvested from managed sustainable forests.

Contents

How promotable are you?

Answer the questions and work out where you are on the promotion scale, then read the guidance points.

Why would you like to get promoted?
a) To have authority.
b) To make a bigger contribution to the organisation.
c) To earn more money.

If a colleague mentioned something to you and then sought your opinion, how would you feel?
a) Very grateful, as it happens rarely.
b) I would appreciate their advice and hope they value my judgement too.
c) I would not listen to their advice, and they should know my opinion already.

If you got promoted, would you treat other members differently from before?
a) No, I would treat them exactly the same.
b) I would try and create an impact on my image to gain more respect and authority.
c) Of course, I would treat them very differently, as they are working for me now.

What kind of approach would you take, in asking for a promotion?

a) I do not have a right to ask and I would wait for them to mention it.

b) I would explain why I should deserve a promotion and any ideas I have for the future.

c) I would insist on a promotion straight away.

How would you impress your managers in order to get a promotion?

a) Always hang around the managers to make sure they notice me.

b) Improve and constantly update my CV. I would also try to appear alert at all times and find out more about ideas behind the networking.

c) I would try to persuade them why I would be ideal for a promotion and express the urgency behind it as well.

Do you think a promotion would affect your family life or other caring responsibilities?

a) Yes, but I am always willing to put my work before anything.

b) I think it will but I will try to balance the two, as I understand more responsibility will be involved.

c) No, I will not let my work overpower crucial time with my family.

If you were to be promoted, how do you think you would change?

a) I would not change because people should respect who I am.

b) I would try and become a more respectable figure.
c) I would not remain friends with any of my colleagues, seeing as I would have such a stressful job and they would be working for me.

a = 1, b = 2, c = 3.
Now add up your scores.

- **8–13**: It is unlikely you are going to be promoted unless you start thinking more positively about yourself. You should always put forward your ideas and let your managers know that you are really interested in a promotion. Also consider that you may have to change some of your qualities when you do get promoted. People will still accept who you are, but will just respect you more as a manager.

- **14–18**: You have a balanced character that will fit perfectly in a manager position. You think of other colleagues and appreciate their advice. Remember to develop your leadership skills in order to express your full potential and achieve your goals.

- **19–24**: Be careful, as you may come across too strong sometimes. Remember to respect other colleagues advice and suggestions instead of always following your own judgement. Also make sure that you treat everyone the same even if you happen to be their manager in the future.

Weighing up the pros and cons of a promotion

If you're thinking about a promotion, you're no doubt a motivated person who wants to play a bigger role in your current company or organisation. In this book, we will discuss ways to reach your goal and make the most of all your potential.

Let's take a step back for a moment. In principle, promotion is a very attractive proposition. It shows that others value your talent and skills and that they want to keep you within the business or organisation. Also enticing are the more tangible benefits of a move up the career ladder: very often a salary increase, a souped-up job title, improved benefits, and so on.

There are lots of positive sides to a promotion, a confidence boost the least among them. Your life may change quite dramatically though, so do take some time to make sure that you've thought about the 'bigger picture' before you launch your campaign.

Step one: Think about your motives

There are many positive reasons to think about promotion. If you're keen to progress in your current field or with your current employer, then clearly it's something that will cross your mind regularly. Promotion means taking on new responsibilities, tackling new challenges, learning new skills, and making a bigger contribution to the organisation as a whole, all of which can be tremendously exciting and a reward for a job well done.

Being promoted can mean, though, that you spend less time doing the job that you've proved your strengths in. For example, let's say you're a graphic designer. You love the creativity that your job affords you and enjoy spending time getting things just right. If you're promoted and become a design manager, your focus may change so that your priority becomes supervising other people's work and you don't get to do much design yourself any more. How would you feel about that? Honestly? If you accept it, fine; but, if you know now that it's not something you'd feel happy about, you're not ready for a move just yet.

Step two: Think about how your working life may change

As mentioned above, hopefully your bank balance will feel the benefit of a promotion, if nothing else! However, it is likely that there'll be more pressure on you in certain areas, and you may also face some situations that you might find tricky on a personal level. For example, you may have to deal with:

- extra work
- extra stress
- longer hours
- less time doing what you love/ what you're good at
- people management responsibilities for the first time
- more complicated internal politics
- being your friend's or partner's boss
- working with powerful people . . . and their egos

TOP TIP

If you have family commitments—whether they be young children or caring responsibilities for older members of your family—do talk to your partner about how he or she may feel about taking on more themselves. If you are the sole carer at home, it's likely you'll need extra help from other sources to keep all your bases covered. Ask friends if they could recommend childminders or other carers who could help: it's always best to find someone via a personal recommendation.

If you're not that confident about your own abilities, you may also find that any feelings of insecurity you have are magnified. On a brighter side, though, you might be excited by the idea of:

- more money
- more status
- satisfying your ambition
- gaining credibility with your peers
- proving others wrong
- a real sense of achievement

TOP TIP

Try not to go for a promotion *solely* for the money. It's always great to have a pay-rise— that goes without saying—but sometimes a wonderful salary can't compensate you for some aspects of a job that you may really not enjoy. Think about what a promotion will do for you in terms of your overall career and don't be forced into applying for something if you just don't want to do it.

Step three: Be ready to put the work in

If you've decided that you want to go for it, the next chapter will help you make yourself promotable. Do realise that you'll need to put some work in: some people are lucky enough to be in the right place at the right time when a great new job comes along but sadly we can't all rely on having that option, so you'll need to make sure that:

- you're cutting the mustard in your existing job
- you look and sound the part
- you're building positive relationships with the right people
- you're ready for the challenge

Long-term promotion campaigns: The 3–1–6–1 plan

If there's no promotion opportunity on the horizon but you know that it's something you want to work towards in the long-term, coming up with a plan—and sticking to it!—is a very effective way of reaching your goals.

To get started, ask yourself what you'd like your life to be like in **three** years' time and write down what comes to mind in as much detail as you can. Write in the present tense, as if it has already happened. Next, repeat this for **one** year's time, **six** months' time and **one** month's time. This '3–1–6–1' plan will help motivate you for the future, as it breaks down the bigger picture of your life into an actionable plan that you can start on right now.

A 'reality check' will help you recognise the right opportunity when it arises, so spend some time on this when you're job-hunting. Divide a page into four quarters, headed:

- Role
- Organisation
- Package
- Boss

Now ask yourself what you want from your next career move. Think about the 'ingredients' that make up your ideal role, putting these into the quadrants on your page. Once your criteria are mapped out in this way, you'll have a visual aid that will help you to weigh up the opportunities that come your way. When you're invited to an interview for a new job, you can use the sheet to come up with strong, targeted questions about the potential role and the organisation.

Good luck!

Common mistakes

✗ You want promotion at all costs

Being recognised professionally is a big achievement and one that can give you a real confidence boost. Do bear in mind, though, that a more senior job can affect your day-to-day life in more ways than one: you may be working longer hours, so it's likely you'll have less time at home than you did before and this may cause friction if you have family commitments. Also, you may find that some of your work friendships change: being the boss is quite a different proposition from being one of the team, however hard you try. Be prepared for changes in all areas of your life.

✗ You don't *do* anything

If promotion is a long-term goal for you, a plan can be a huge help, as it works by provoking specific and related actions which together create the desired effect. There's absolutely no point, however, in writing a plan, carrying out the first action, and then leaving it to gather dust. You have to be ready to keep plugging away at your to-do list in order to get a good result. You may get downhearted at times but try to keep setbacks in perspective and to keep your goal in sight.

STEPS TO SUCCESS

✔ Winning a promotion is a great achievement and a fitting reward for a job well done. Promotion can, though, affect more areas of your life than just your work; so do make sure you've thought about the bigger picture before you decide to go for it.

✔ Make sure you want to be promoted for the right reasons. A bigger salary is wonderful, of course, but it might not compensate you enough for working for the boss from hell or giving up all your weekends.

✔ Think about how a possible promotion might affect those you are close to. For example, if you have children or othor caring responsibilities, you may need to ask others to help you out more or you may even need to rethink your current arrangements completely. The last thing you want is to come home from a new, potentially more stressful job to find more strife at home, so talk to your partner or family members about your plans first.

✔ Be ready to change your 'persona' at work. It's hard to go from being one of the team to being the boss, but that is something you'll have to get used to as you work in more senior positions.

✔ Be prepared to put in extra work to make yourself an excellent promotion candidate. Turn to the next chapter for more help.

✔ If promotion is something you're working towards long-term, put together your own 3–1–6–1 plan. It's a very useful way of breaking down the bigger picture of your life into small action plans you can start working on now.

✔ If you do put together a plan, stick to it!

Useful links

iVillage.co.uk:
www.ivillage.co.uk
TotalJobs.com:
www.totaljobs.com

Making yourself promotable

These days, being good at your job doesn't automatically mean that you'll get promoted. Being *promotable,* on the other hand, increases your chances of success and helps you take the career steps you're aiming for.

Being promotable draws together your professional skills, competence, business sense, and relationship-building skills. The result? The impression of someone who will be valuable to your organisation at increasingly senior levels. When you're recognised for your specialist expertise and have a track record of success, you're no doubt likely to be seen as a candidate who can move up through the ranks. You will need other personal attributes that go well beyond your current role, though. To get ahead, you'll need to show that you have good business sense, can deal with the trials of office politics and are able to manage change, and that you're loyal to your employer to boot.

These attributes go hand-in-hand with the need to communicate and network effectively, and you'll also need to cement good links with people who can sponsor and support you as you move along your career path. Don't worry if this sounds

like a tall order: read on to find out how you can
bring all your skills together and make them work
for you.

Step one: Work on your 'visibility'

**1 I'm very keen to be promoted and think I have
done everything I can to get noticed.
Competition is fierce, though, so how can I
boost my chances?**

Blowing your own trumpet too loudly isn't always the most
effective way of influencing events. Being clear about what
you want and why you deserve to be promoted is, of course,
very important, but a subtle approach can also reap
rewards. You could, for example:

- find a mentor or sponsor in the organisation with whom
  you can work (see chapter 7 for more help on this)
- talk to your boss and discuss your development plan,
  emphasising that you believe you have more to offer the
  business

Remember that you don't have to limit your campaign just to
your office space. Why not publish articles in your trade or
professional magazine, or accept invitations (or volunteer) to
speak at conferences? If you want to raise your visibility
more locally to demonstrate your commitment to your local
area, you could get involved in a charity or community
initiative.

TOP TIP
Try to become more visible by taking the
opportunity to mix with decision-makers and
by sharing stories of your success at
appropriate times. It is quite a tricky
balancing act, as you don't want to annoy the
very people you're trying to get to know, so
use your common sense and judge the
situation before you start spreading the good
news about yourself! For example, don't
chase people round the office to tell them
something when they're clearly in a rush or in
a bad mood.

---

2 I work in an organisation where promotion is a thing of the past for most people. How can I work my way into the senior management tier?

Many modern businesses have opted for 'flatter'
management structures and this means that there's often
no longer a clear 'route to the top'. In cases like these,
'promotability' has to come from a different angle. For
example, there may be prestigious and exciting areas for
you to work in, or some career-enhancing assignments
that you could get involved with.

TOP TIP
Every business has its own way of doing
things or a distinct set of criteria by which it
measures its high-flyers. Take a step back and
see if you can spot why other people in your
organisation have been promoted. Is it a
reward for what they've achieved, or the way
they've done it? If you can spot a trend, you'll
be able to plan how to follow it yourself.

Step two: Think about the bigger picture for a moment

Making yourself promotable is not an easy task because it means that you have impress on many different fronts. For example, you have to be familiar with not just your own organisation, but with what's going on in other areas of your industry. What are the trends? If you work for a commercial organisation, is your market thriving or shrinking?

You need to develop social and political skills so that you can build good relationships with others and also find a personal leadership style that you're comfortable with and can develop into a distinctive personal 'brand' in the long run.

It's ironic that you may find that the personal skills and attributes that have helped you reach your current rung on the career ladder might actually sabotage your chances to climb any further. For example, if you have a very individualistic approach that differentiates you from your peers or are seen as a 'maverick' prone to challenging the status quo, you might have to think about losing such traits. This may not appeal to everyone, so do think long and hard about the changes you might have to make—and how you'd feel about yourself in the process—before you embark on your campaign.

Research conducted by the Academy of Management in the late 1990s highlighted several extra factors that can prevent otherwise very capable people from progressing in their careers. These include:

- problems with building good relationships with others
- not meeting business objectives
- failure to build and lead a team
- not being able to change, or cope with change

Two further derailment factors that were considered to reflect the changing business environment were later identified. These were the failure to *learn* to deal with change and complexity and overdependence upon a single boss or mentor.

If you work at each of these factors in turn, you'll be building the personal capabilities that will boost your promotability and distinguish you as a future leader.

Step three: Build great interpersonal skills

As you progress through your career, there's a shift in the balance between the skills you have to offer and your ability to build relationships. This latter talent becomes an important part of your personal work 'armoury'—more senior roles demand a higher level of political sensitivity because at that level relationships go beyond the day-to-day work setting and are more likely have an impact on the long-term interests of the business.

Knowing this, many potential leaders try to fake it with an over-confident communication style. Don't go there. An approach like this will just make you seem arrogant and unlikeable.

TOP TIP

Good interpersonal relationships are built by people who have no axe to grind and who aren't trying to create an illusion of confidence and capability. There's no substitute for genuine self-confidence; people can generally see through those who are putting it on, so make sure you know yourself well, understand your values, and can create a clear picture of what you want.

**With this in place, good communication and
an easy manner will follow naturally and
authoritatively because it will genuinely
reflect who you are.**

Step four: Meet your objectives

To be promotable, not only do you have to meet the
objectives of your role, but you have to contribute to the
wider business too. This means showing initiative and
taking an interest in areas outside your role boundaries.
You could do this by volunteering for an important project,
chairing a committee, or leading a special interest group. If
you're seen to be supportive of—and passionate about—the
business, you're much more likely to be noticed as
someone who could make an impact at a more senior
level.

Although it might be unpalatable to some, you may have to
consider (subtle) ways in which you can broadcast your
willingness to play a more committed part in the fortunes of
your business, such as suggesting or volunteering for a
special project. This doesn't mean that you have to be
sycophantic, but, if you act like someone who occupies the
type of role you're aiming for, it'll be easy for others to see
you in that role.

TOP TIP

There's absolutely no point blowing your own trumpet if you can't show that you're meeting your targets regularly and effectively. Nothing is as impressive as a job well done, so get the basics right and then build on them.

Step five: Build and lead teams

Being able to build and lead teams is an essential skill for senior executives. Without this, the co-operative networks that are vital for an organisation to achieve its objectives are damaged. Your success in this area depends on how well you can communicate clear objectives as well as understand the skills, motivations, and personal values of your team.

Good working relationships are open, with a healthy ebb and flow of feedback to make sure that everyone knows what the team's purpose and goals are. Build in milestones and markers to your work plan so that you can monitor progress and—just as importantly—celebrate success. It's an excellent way of motivating others.

Step six: Learn to manage transition and change

Businesses and organisations have to respond to developments in markets and economies, and the ripple-effects of these changes have an impact on all employees. Being able to field such changes and use your knowledge and insight to direct people's creative energy towards making them a success are valuable attributes of a leader. Being unable—or unwilling—to embrace change, on the other hand, even if you feel the change is unwise or counter-productive, could be seen as being unhelpful.

If you find yourself in a situation like this, rather than just putting up the shutters and making your displeasure clear to all, take a more constructive approach by making some alternative suggestions and explaining the thinking behind them. If your concerns are rejected, though, and you still want to stay with the company, you'll have to combat your reservations and show your loyalty by remaining flexible and actively seeking ways of making the changes work.

Show that you're prepared to keep people motivated and learn from the new experience rather than bang on about how unhappy you feel about it. In short, remaining flexible and looking for practical ways of making (sometimes difficult) things happen, keeping people motivated, and learning from it are all important characteristics of those in the top team.

Step seven: Build an effective network of champions or sponsors

We've all seen people who have been promoted on the basis of who they know, not what they know, yet this is no guarantee of future success. Indeed, sheltering under someone's protective wing is all very well when your champion is in favour, but, if their reputation is damaged for any reason, yours will also be tarnished because of your close association.

To avoid this, build a robust network of relationships that will support you purely because of your potential and personal integrity. In this way, you can be sure that you aren't reliant on the perception people have of someone else (and over whom you have no control), but that you're judged on your own talent and attributes.

Can you identify role-models, potential coaches, and mentors among your colleagues who could help with your development plan? Frame your requests for help positively and explain that you feel you have more to offer the business and would appreciate their guidance—try not to phrase it so that it seems that you're more bothered about yourself than the organisation. Turn to chapter 6 for more advice on this issue.

Common mistakes

✗ You irritate the people who could help you

Sometimes, people looking for a move up the career ladder make such a fuss about their ambitions that they make a lot of noise around the people who they think can promote them. This won't help their case, and in fact it's very irritating and counter-productive. There are unwritten 'rules' to being promotable, which change from company to company, and you need to work these out by observing and adopting some of the tactics of successful people who've gone before you. Find out about the interests of those at the top and show that you're interested in them too, or make yourself known in their philanthropic circles outside the business. For example, if you know that your boss supports a local charity, society, or sports team, why not go along to one of their events?

✗ You're not willing to change

Although a track record of being a maverick may get you noticed, this is usually not a trait that will get you promoted. If you are hoping for a promotion, it's probably worth playing down your notoriety and redirecting your energies into activities that support the organisation's best interests. Do think long and hard about how comfortable you feel about trying this route, however. For many people, there's nothing worse than not being able to be themselves.

✗ You ignore your team

It's tempting to focus on yourself as you look towards your career horizon and plan for your own success. You'll be judged on your ability to develop the talent in your team, though, so don't ignore them. You won't succeed by squashing those with potential, so you must trust in your own abilities and let your team flourish too. Doing this will create a loyal group who will support you in the long run. Take care to maintain these relationships as you move through the organisation, as you never know who you'll be working with (or for!) one day.

STEPS TO SUCCESS

✔ Understand that being 'promotable' means having a mix of the right skills and personal attributes.

✔ To get a fix on what makes someone promotable in your organisation, observe the people who have climbed up the career ladder already and work out how they've done it.

✔ If you're on good terms with people who've been successful in this way at work, ask for their suggestions on your next move. Always thank them for their time and ask if there's anything you can help them with: this is the secret of good networking.

✔ Don't alienate the people who could help you most. You'll need the help of mentors and advisers in your campaign, so don't harass them, or bang on at great length or at the wrong time. Use your common sense to pick a good moment to talk about your promotion dreams.

✔ Be prepared to go the extra mile. Raising your profile outside your work setting can often boost your visibility at the office. Take up opportunities to speak at events, write for external publications, or work with your local community.

✔ Show you can deliver. There's no point blowing your own trumpet if you don't meet your business objectives. Don't expect others to take you seriously if you can't come up with the goods.

✔ If you manage a team already, don't sacrifice them to your own ambition. You have a job to do in leading them every day.

Useful links

Dauten.com:
www.dauten.com/promotable.htm
OCJobSite.com:
www.ocjobsite.com/job-articles/promote-yourself.asp

Developing presence

Presence is an elusive human quality, but one that can really boost your chances of success during your promotion campaign. Meeting your objectives and showing that you're good at what you do are clearly extremely important aspects of a successful career, but presence enables someone to command respect—or at least attention—so it's something that you need to think about.

Some people believe you're born with presence, or charisma, while others think that it develops as a by-product of success. In fact, it's probably a combination of the two—and almost anyone can certainly nurture and develop it in themselves. It most often seems to result from confidence in what you're doing, when you feel at home with, or passionate about, your role. Presence is most likely to elude us when we're not sure of ourselves and feeling uncomfortable, so job interviews and other stressful promotion situations are times when it might be hard to conjure it up. With some practice, though, and a belief in your own abilities, you can seem much more confident than you may feel!

Step one: Don't hold yourself back

'Presence' is one of those words that makes the more unassuming among us think 'I couldn't possibly do that'. But don't dismiss it out of hand, and do try to see how working on this aspect of your professional 'armour' really can help you. As you'll see in chapters 6 and 7, business runs on relationships, so anything you can do to help yourself to make an impression on others will be very positive.

TOP TIP

Before we go any further, let's dispel one misapprehension: having presence has nothing at all to do with how tall you are. There are many successful political and business leaders who have compensated for their lack of stature in other ways—Gandhi, Mother Theresa, Nelson Mandela, and Napoleon are just a few examples. Presence can be created by a state of mind: the adage 'think tall and you will be tall' really does work.

Don't worry if you find that you command attention in some areas of your life but are less successful at work. This happens a lot: people who are happy and confident in one setting find they can't 'switch on' their talent in a different setting. There are some useful techniques that will enable you to transfer your talents between situations, though, and one that seems to work very well is 'anchoring'. Briefly, it relies on your ability to capture the feeling when you're doing something really well and associate it with a gesture, movement, or saying—such as pinching your thumb and forefinger together. This becomes the 'anchor', and, when you transfer your anchor into a new setting, all the memories of performing well flood back and allow you to do so at will.

On a similar theme, some managers worry that, although they have real credibility with their team members, they don't make the same positive impression on their peers or managers. If you feel you're in this situation, try not to worry. Remember that with the people who work for you you have three things that they don't: knowledge, expertise, and authority. When you're with your peers and managers, they probably have the same or more of these things—or create the illusion that they do. This can be sufficiently intimidating to make you lose your confidence. Try the 'anchor' technique described above to see if you can transfer your confidence into encounters with your peers and managers.

Step two: Understand the four key areas of presence

1 Physical

This refers to how you manage your body. People with presence often have good posture, even if they're small. They stand and move well, projecting calm and confidence.

Being fit and in good general health are key factors. Exercise, good diet, and proper rest are important allies, as are 'centring' practices like meditation and yoga, even though they may not be for everyone. Good quality clothes that fit well emphasise posture and confidence. They don't need to be expensive or conventional, just carefully chosen to suit the occasion.

Non-verbal behaviour can reinforce the impression you're trying to create. Steady eye contact, a clear voice, and appropriate gestures are powerful channels of non-verbal communication. People with presence also often create the impression of being larger than they actually are, by the clever use of space. If sitting, they may sit with one arm resting on the back of the chair, their body at an angle, and one leg crossed over the other. This position takes up a large amount of space and is very confident and imposing. Look for opportunities to project a 'bigger' persona; use fuller, sweeping arm movements, rather than just a hand or pointing finger. It's a good idea to practise in front of a mirror or a friend until you get used to them, so that you won't overdo them in public.

2 Mental/emotional

The mind is one of the most important tools for creating presence, and the technique of visualisation is a very successful one: our thoughts always precede our actions and behaviour; so, by making your intention explicit in your mind, you'll already be creating it in reality. For example:

TOP TIP
The ability to build rapport is invaluable.
Good eye contact when engaging with people,
even if in an audience, enables you to make
valuable human impressions. Paying proper
attention to what people say and
demonstrating that you've heard their
comments is important. So, too, is
remembering people, and the context in
which you know them. By deliberately using
someone's name when you're speaking to
them, you can embed it in your mind.

✓ Visualise yourself as a person who emanates
presence.

✓ See your picture in colour; examine it in detail.

✓ Note the feelings that arise in you, the sound of an
audience applauding, the glow of achievement as you
make your exit.

✓ Make positive affirmations: 'I am confident', 'I feel good',
'I have presence'. These will train your brain to believe
what you see in your mind's eye.

✓ Repeat your positive affirmations regularly so that they
become the dominant messages that you transmit about
yourself.

TOP TIP
Make sure these positive messages to
yourself are in the present tense. If you say 'I
will be confident', your brain will believe it to
be a *future* scenario, and you may never get
there!

---

3 Mastery

Know your stuff. All the knowledge and experience you've
built up during your career will let you be confident in what
you say and do. Make sure people know your worth and
what a catch you are by being open and honest; share your
experiences subtly, tell stories, and try to build real
relationships with others. Try not to take over, though: very
often, people on a quest to create presence for themselves
stop seeing and listening to others. Try to be inclusive, and
'generosity' will also become part of your presence.

Mastering all these elements will open new doors of
opportunity for you: people will gravitate to you, offer you
new leadership roles, and spread the good word about your
qualities and skills.

4 Occasion

People with presence are able to create a sense of occasion
in even the most ordinary of circumstances, such as walking
along the production line, chairing a meeting, or giving a
presentation.

Presence is about transmitting a quality that others trust and respond to. It makes them feel as if they're gaining something just from being close to you. If it's to be sustained, having presence carries quite a lot of responsibility. For those who look up to you, you'll be providing guidance and inspiring confidence, reflecting their values, and—perhaps—being their conscience.

Common mistakes

✗ You mistake over-confidence for presence

These two traits are absolutely not the same thing. Over-confidence is all about yourself; presence is about others. Over-confident people can come across as self-interested and unempathic, whereas someone with presence is often seen as taking an interest and building relationships. Those who seem to be over-confident are actually very often insecure, and are trying to compensate for this.

✗ You think that presence can't be developed

Having a certain amount of natural presence is a gift, yes, but it's one that needs attention and development to mature properly. Look for occasions where you can practise the techniques that will help you project the impression you seek. By building up a series of successes, you'll soon be able to join them together and emanate this quality at will. In time, it may become second nature.

✗ You aren't fully prepared

As discussed above, there are physical, mental, emotional, mastery, and 'occasion' elements involved in presence. It's important to have them all working in harmony—if you don't, you could ruin all your good work. For example, imagine looking good, having a clear intention, having the occasion . . . but nothing to say. Or conversely, having a great story or bit of information, but getting the timing all wrong. Each element assists and supports the others, so pay careful attention to all of them.

STEPS TO SUCCESS

✔ If you're a shy person, don't assume that presence is something that will always elude you; you can develop it with a little effort.

✔ If you find it easier to command respect in some areas of your life than others, there are lots of effective techniques you can use to transfer your skills between different settings. 'Anchoring' is particularly useful.

✔ There are four key areas of presence, all of which need to work in harmony, as they back each other up. They are: physical, mental/emotional, mastery, and occasion.

✔ Physical presence comes from the way you manage your body. Make sure you have good posture, uso 'open' body language, and keep up good eye contact.

✔ Your mind can help you boost your presence via the use of positive visualisation techniques. If you 'see' yourself behaving and being recognised in the way you'd like, you'll naturally act as if this is so.

✔ Mastery comes from knowing your stuff. Let the experience you've built up during your career boost your confidence. Share your experiences subtly and remember to let others have their say too.

✔ Don't think that over-confidence and presence are the same thing—they're anything but. Over-confident people seem remote and self-absorbed; those with presence take an interest in others and actively build positive, warm relationships.

Useful links

Mental Health Net—Center Site, LLC (Ohio, USA):
http://mentalhelp.net/psyhelp/chap14/chap14b.htm
Mind Tools (London):
www.mindtools.com

Managing your image: How to create an impact

Along with increasing your visibility in the office, managing your image can really help you in your quest for promotion. It's not something that many of us would automatically think about, but canny image management can increase the confidence people place in you and the career opportunities that come your way.

It starts, as you'd imagine, with the first impression you make. Perceptions are remarkably difficult to dislodge once they're in place, so do think about the kind of impact you want to create from the outset and how you can achieve this. If you can get this right, it'll be much less complicated to manage your image in the longer term.

Step one: Understand how managing your image can help you at work

Before we go any further, don't think that managing your image means that you can't be yourself. In fact, it's anything but that. To put across the best possible impression of yourself, you have to feel comfortable with everything you say and do, or people will pick up on it and think you're putting on an act. Image management is merely presenting yourself in the best light, not a false light. We all exercise some control over the way we behave in different situations—this is just another instance in which conscious control can bring advantages.

TOP TIP

Creating a good impression isn't size or shape dependent, thankfully—just think of some of the most successful business people, politicians, or celebrities! A good impression is created through your intention and the way you feel about yourself. Try portraying yourself in different ways in front of a mirror and see what a difference it makes to the way your body responds. Your body language follows your thoughts. Get your thoughts right, and you'll have no problem.

You can even create a good impression when you're feeling under pressure. The best way to do this is to try and 'tune in' to the expectations of the other people you may be meeting. For example, if you have to give an important presentation, do some useful preparation work beforehand. Check who will be in the audience and anticipate what sorts of questions will be asked of you so that you can cope with whatever's thrown at you—include some worst-case scenarios as well! Rehearse your presentation, be confident about your material, and feel comfortable in what you're going to wear. If you feel inside that you're successful, you'll behave as if you are and convey that impression to others too.

TOP TIP

It can be difficult to judge how you're coming across to others and you may be worried that you're trying too hard. If this is the case, take a step back and observe people who naturally manage their image well. You can pick up useful clues from their behaviour. Also ask for feedback and advice from people you trust on what you could do more successfully.

Step two: Understand the five Cs

It's said that an impression is created in the first seven seconds of meeting someone and that, once that impression is made, it's hard to change it. You need to think about how to make those vital few seconds work for you, and thinking about the 'five Cs' can help. They are:

- context
- communication
- credibility
- clothing
- composure/confidence

1 Context

First of all, be aware of the context you find yourself in. Understand the purpose of the occasion, the agendas of those present, and the circumstances surrounding the situation. Whether you're being interviewed for a job or conducting an important client meeting, spend some time thinking about what your audience's expectations are and how you can meet these. For example, is it an occasion where you should go out on a limb to distinguish yourself from others, or is it a time when you need to show how well you can fit in to the established order of things?

2 Communication—verbal and non-verbal

Once you understand the kind of occasion you're facing, think about what you're going to say—and how you're going to say it. Good communicators are able to adjust the tone, tenor, and timing of their speech to make the maximum impact.

Neurolinguistic programming (NLP) has a great deal to say on this subject. It recommends listening closely to the kinds of words that other people use so that you can better understand the way they interpret and represent the world. This divides into five different arenas: visual, kinaesthetic, auditory, gustatory, and olfactory, with the first three being the most common.

For example, some people 'see' things in their mind's eye and say things like: 'I can see what you're saying' or 'I have a clear vision of what this will look like'. Others make 'sense' of the world through movement, touch, and feelings, and use phrases that describe a sense or movement, such as: 'I feel very positive about this' or 'The change in the market may mean a crushing blow to the business'. People who have an auditory approach will say things like, 'I hear what you're saying' or 'It sounds suspicious to me!'

Whenever you meet someone or a group of people, take some time to listen carefully to what they say so that you can find out which type of language appeals to them most—visual, kinaesthetic, or auditory—or at least use a mixture of the three so that there is something there for everyone. Compatible language and body language gives the impression of immediate rapport, which is enormously helpful in creating an impact.

On this note, do make sure that your body language is consistent with what you're saying. If you don't believe in your message, your body will show it somehow and this

---

TOP TIP

To make an excellent impact when you're giving a presentation, speak clearly and enunciate your words properly so that everyone can hear you without having to strain. Stand tall and remember that the speed, tone, and pitch of your voice are all signals that will be picked up by your audience.

---

mismatch is called *leakage*, You often see it when people are nervous or are saying something they know to be untrue. You'll see their feet shifting, a knee jiggling, or exaggerated gestures as they try to compensate for their discomfort with their own words.

3 Credibility

Don't bluff. Make sure you know your stuff and that you have a few (true!) examples to drop into conversation to show the depth of your knowledge. Many of us have been trained as children not to blow our own trumpets or boast about our achievements, but in a work context—especially if you're hoping to get noticed—you need to find opportunities to show your experience and skills. To do this, make connections with what others say and use them as openings to illustrate your own experiences. For example, if you agree with what someone has said, you could say 'Yes, I know what you mean. I found that when I . . . '.

Do take care not to overdo things, though. Make sure you listen carefully to others rather than just lurk on the edges of a conversation trying to say your piece. Obviously you want to tell others about your achievements, but you need to do it in a way that enhances their opinion of you, not that detracts from it. Just as importantly, show an interest in other people and don't hog the limelight.

TOP TIP
Even if there are lots of people you are
desperate to make contact with at a particular
event, don't start looking over the shoulder of
the person or persons you're speaking to in
order to see who you might want to move on
to next. However hard you try to mask your
social rubbernecking, others will notice and
won't be impressed.

---

4 Clothing

What you wear can enhance or destroy a first impression. Too much of a good thing can be a disaster: too bright, too tight, too sexy—extremes will paint a picture of you that will stay in the observer's mind.

What to wear largely depends upon the situation. The safest strategy is to reflect the style of those that you'll be meeting, perhaps erring on the side of conservatism. If you work in (or are hoping to work in) a less traditional setting, you have the freedom to be a bit more creative, but if you're working in a reasonably traditional corporate setting, it's best to reflect that in your clothes.

Good grooming is equally vital. Make sure that you're well turned out. Try to avoid dark wet patches under your arms, an unironed shirt or blouse, and food-stained clothes. Clean and tidy is the best bet for most occasions.

5 Composure/confidence

Composure comes from confidence. When you're sure of what you want and are well prepared, you'll feel confident and seem composed to others. This will allow you to manage any unexpected turns in the situation without a problem.

Once you've created a good impact, you'll find it relatively easy to maintain. Just as bad impressions are hard to displace, so are good impressions. If you invest in getting it right first time, you won't have to concern yourself with how to change the impression at a later date.

Common mistakes

✗ You try too hard at first

Image management is a subtle skill. A common mistake is to try too hard, exaggerating your natural characteristics in order to convey confidence. Try practising in front of a friend or trusted colleague and ask for feedback on the impression you're creating. Be open to trying something different. If you're embarrassed to do this, try it in front of a mirror. You won't get feedback as such, but mirrors never lie!

✗ You leave it to chance

You can inadvertently create a poor image by expecting people to know where your talents or intentions lie without actually telling them. You have to engage actively in creating an image. If you want others to know about something, find a way of weaving it subtly into the conversation. Provide your audience with a hook that they can remember you by. If you 'project' bland, you may be remembered as bland. Or you may not be remembered at all!

✗ You go too far accidentally

Misreading a situation and drawing attention to yourself in a negative way can be difficult to recover from. If this happens, you may find it best to declare your mistake and start again. Few people can come up smelling of roses and rally in situations like this.

✗ You forget that other people have networks

Do remember that the impressions you make on others will travel beyond your immediate audience. Each person you meet has a network; so, if you create a good impression, word will spread round that network and you could reap the rewards. If you're indiscreet or misjudge a situation, the 'bad' news will travel just as fast, if not faster. Bear in mind that you aren't meeting just one person, or a few people, but in a 'virtual' sense, their close acquaintances too.

STEPS TO SUCCESS

✔ Managing your image can be a real help if you're trying to get yourself noticed during your promotion campaign.

✔ Don't see image management as trying to be something—or someone—you're not, but rather as a way of showing yourself and your skills in the best light.

✔ To make a good impression on someone, try to tune in to his or her expectations or outlook on the world.

✔ Listen carefully to the language that other people use and use similar phrases that will have resonance with them—they'll immediately feel that you're on the same wavelength.

✔ While it's important to let other people know what your strengths are, use your common sense about how and when to talk about yourself. Judge the occasion carefully, be brief, and remember to ask people about themselves too. It's a conversation, not a monologue!

✔ If you're worried about how you might be coming across to others, ask a friend or trusted colleague for some feedback. If you feel that people are misunderstanding you, it could be simply that you're trying too hard and inadvertently coming across as 'false'.

✔ Think about the 5 Cs when you're trying to make a good impression on someone: context, communication, credibility, clothing, and composure/confidence.

✔ Make sure your body language is consistent with what you say: it's easy to tell if you feel uncomfortable with what you're saying (even though you might think you've got away with it).

Useful links

HRM Guide—performance management and the organisation:
www.hrmguide.co.uk/hrm/chap10/ch10-links2.htm#ch10-imp
Mind Tools (London):
www.mindtools.com

Standing out from the crowd: Knock-out applications

Now that you've been working on your own skills and getting yourself into promotable shape, the next thing you need to do is make a splash when you see a promotion opportunity that really appeals to you.

This is your chance to shine, so make sure you do yourself justice by conveying your skills and experience to the best possible advantage. There are two main ways of applying for a new job: CV with covering letter, and application form.

Step one: Get to grips with application forms

Some organisations, especially those in the public sector, often invite applicants to fill in an application form. They can put some people off, but remember, this is a chance to show your experience and skills, so don't be put off by a prescriptive format.

There are things you can to do to make filling in the form less of a chore.

1 Give yourself plenty of time to complete the form: if you feel rushed, you're more likely to make a mistake. If you only have a hard copy of the form, photocopy it and work on the copy rather than launch straight into the real thing.

2 Check the deadline!

3 Before you start, read through the entire form carefully so that you can plan where to place information and don't end up repeating yourself.

4 Read the instructions and follow them! If you don't, the person reading it may take a dim view of your application, despite your match of skills, and file it in the bin.

5 Answer every question accurately or at least write 'not applicable' so that the recruiter knows that you haven't missed it by mistake. Remember that application forms and CVs are often checked to make sure the information is true, so don't be tempted to embroider your work history.

6 Do proof-read your draft application form after a day or two: it's amazing what you spot with a little distance. Even better, ask a trusted colleague, friend, or family member to read it as well as back-up. When you're

completely satisfied with what you've written, transfer it onto the original form.

7 Save the final version somewhere safe if you're working electronically or photocopy it if you're posting it back. It may be a month or more before you're asked to attend an interview and you'll need to remind yourself of what you wrote.

8 Make sure you return it in plenty of time.

Step two: Revitalise your CV

There are quite a few different types of CV, but a traditional chronological one is probably the best one to use for this occasion as it shows your track record of achievements.

TOP TIP

Do make an effort to update your CV when you apply for a new job—especially a promotion—and don't just dust off an old one you have to hand. It's a great opportunity to list new skills and experience you've gained, so don't waste it.

Try to keep your CV short: one or two pages of A4 is fine. Any more, and the recruiter will lose interest. Remember that you don't need to give a blow-by-blow account of everything you've ever done; if you're applying for an internal promotion the potential interviewers are likely to know that anyway, but you can give additional information once you get to speak to them in person. The trick is to get the reader thinking of questions that they would like to ask you. For example, you could talk about an achievement and the impact that it had on your department but hold back the information about how you did it, leaving this as a 'hook'.

Keep the structure of your CV clean so that the reader's attention isn't distracted from all your experience and achievements:

1 Write your name and contact details at the top. If you're not applying for a vacancy at your current employer, don't give your work e-mail address: it looks unprofessional and gives the impression that you're misusing your current employer's facilities. Use your home e-mail address, if you have one, or a Web-based e-mail provider such as Hotmail or Yahoo.

2 List your employment history. Start with your present or most recent position and work backwards.

3 For each position listed, describe your major duties and accomplishments, beginning with an action verb. Highlight your achievements.

4 Keep your career goals in mind as you write and, as you describe your duties and accomplishments, emphasise those which are most related to the job you're hoping to get.

5 Include your education in a separate section at the bottom of your CV. If you have more than one degree, list them in reverse chronological order. Also list any professional qualifications or relevant training you've undertaken separately.

TOP TIP

Remember that you need to grab attention in the first half page of A4, so don't waste this section listing your middle names, marital status, and date of birth. These items can be left out or put at the end of the second page. Make the most important information readily accessible, and remove irrelevant information. An hour carefully tailoring your CV can prove to be well spent.

Step three: Write a great covering letter

If you're applying for your promotion with a CV, you'll need a knock-out covering letter to go with it too. 'Letter' is a bit of a misnomer these days, as many applications are sent with a covering e-mail, but the principle is the same: whatever medium you use, the covering letter is the first thing a recruiter or manager will read, so it needs to make an impact. It's your first chance to stand out from the crowd and make the reader want to meet you.

TOP TIP
**Always make sure that your letter is
addressed to someone in particular, rather
than to a catch-all 'Dear Sir/Madam'. Firstly, it
will mean that your letter will arrive with the
right person more quickly, and, secondly, it'll
show that you've bothered to find out who you
need to contact. Most advertisements do give
a contact name, but, if you're not sure who to
write to, do some investigation on your target
company's website or call their reception to
find out.**

Say why you're writing

Most promotions are existing, advertised vacancies.
Begin your letter by describing the position that interests
you and explain in the first sentence why you're writing.
You could also say where you saw the vacancy. For
example:

I am very interested in the position of Production Manager
as described in your advertisement of 22 June on the
Daily Post website.

Alternatively, if you're writing following a recommendation
from someone else working at or known to the company,
make that clear:

I have been given your name by Ms Mary Robertson
regarding the position of Human Resources manager.

2 Show you're interested

Take time to show you've done your homework and that you
understand what the company does and what its aims are.
Even if you're applying for a different job at your current
employer, you can still do this. Show that you understand
new challenges the business is facing or how it's trying to
break into new markets, for example.

You can find out this type of useful information by visiting the
company's website and reading any relevant press
coverage. Press releases are a great source of information.
Also read through the relevant trade press so that you can
see how the company you're interested in fits into the wider
scene.

Finally, to get across the fact that you've read the job
advertisement properly and have understood it, match the
language you use in your letter to the advertisement itself.
For example, if the job description refers to a 'team leader',
repeat that job title in your correspondence rather than using
the word 'manager' instead.

3 Tell them why they need *you*

Explain why you're an excellent candidate for this job early
in the letter so that you grab your reader's interest. A

good way of doing this is explaining how, in your current job, you've helped your company reach its goals. For example:

I understand that your company is planning to create a Web presence to support sales. In my current position as director of international sales for Speedy Sales Company, I have helped increase our market share by 13% in the past year.

TOP TIP

Be as accurate as you can! There's no point embroidering your achievements, as, if you're offered the job and your references are taken up, your new employer is bound to pick up on any discrepancies.

---

4 Suggest an interview

You can do this by telling your reader that you'll be in his or her area at a particular time and that you'd be available for interview then. If you're more comfortable with a less direct approach, you can simply say 'I look forward to discussing how my experience can help your organisation to be more successful'.

5 Remember the essentials

✔ Keep your covering letter short and to the point. An effective covering letter is usually only two or three paragraphs long.

✔ Be yourself. CVs are factual records of your experiences and skills. A good covering letter is your chance to show your personality and stand out from the crowd of other applicants as the interview short-list is drawn up. Keep the letter professional, but don't be afraid to show your enthusiasm, your willingness to work hard, and your interest in the position. Potential employers want job applicants who show an interest in them and who seem eager to be a part of their company.

✔ Make sure your covering letter looks professional, check that there are no spelling or grammatical errors, and read it carefully before you send it off. If possible, ask someone else to read over it for you too.

✔ As with your CV, if you're posting it to a recruiter, use the best quality paper you can afford. Stick to white or ivory-coloured paper unless you're applying for a creative post.

✔ Use a standard or easily readable font such as Times New Roman or Arial.

✔ If you're posting your letter and CV, send them in a large flat envelope. You might want to send two copies in case

the recruiter wants to show them to colleagues:
photocopies or scans will be clearer if the originals
haven't been folded.

✔ If you're e-mailing your letter and CV, double-check that
you have definitely attached the relevant files before you
send the e-mail! Also be ready to send your files in a
different format in case the recipient has difficulty
opening them.

Common mistakes

✗ You don't read the application form properly

Do take time to read through an application form from
beginning to end before you start to fill it in. Now that
many application forms are e-mailed to candidates, the
problem is not so much that you have only one to work
from and might mess it up, but that you just don't think
carefully about how best to phrase your application and
lose an excellent opportunity to shine.

✗ You can't be bothered to update your CV

If you want to get a promotion, you are going to have to
put some effort in, and updating your CV is time very well
spent. It's one of the best ways of showcasing your
talents and experience, so make sure you polish up your
CV to show what you've achieved at work. Begin all the
descriptions of your current and previous jobs with an
action verb, such as 'managed', 'achieved', 'secured',
or 'improved'.

✗ You use a covering letter template from a book

Reading through examples of covering letters from a book of templates can help you understand what to include and how to lay out and phrase your letter. Do remember to customise the basic format so that it fits your needs specifically. No manager or recruiter will want to hear the same tired old phrases that they've heard so often before.

STEPS TO SUCCESS

✔ Apply for promotion opportunities in good time. If you leave things to the last minute, you're much more likely to make a mistake, as you'll have been rushing.

✔ Whatever application method you're asked to use, do your homework about the company you're writing to so that you can show you understand their challenges and successes.

✔ If you need to use an application form and are given a hard copy to fill in, take a photocopy before you start so that you can plan how best to fill it in.

✔ If you're applying with a CV and cover letter, make sure that both are tailored carefully to suit the needs of your target company: don't just dig out old documents that you've used before.

✔ Let your enthusiasm for the advertised job shine through.

✔ Show how your experience and skills can help your target company or organisation achieve greater success.

✔ Proof-read your letter and CV or application form before you send it in for consideration. Even better, ask someone else to read it over for you: we tend to 'agree' with ourselves, so someone else's perspective will be very useful.

✔ If you're applying for an advertised vacancy, check that you've given all the information that the advertisement requested. If the recruiters want to know your current salary and notice period, make sure you've mentioned them.

✔ Make sure you have a copy of your application so that you can refresh your memory before an interview.

Useful link

Monster Careers:
www.monster.co.uk

Networking and marketing yourself

Whatever your current job, whatever your career goals, you can always benefit from networking and marketing yourself. Business today is driven by relationships. Networking and marketing yourself require you to build strong and meaningful relationships—many that will be long term and some that may be extremely helpful as you look for promotion opportunities.

Before you plunge in, ask yourself the following questions:

- Why am I networking? What's my personal or professional goal?
- What are my strengths that will help me to market myself?
- What organisations or events will be valuable places for networking?
- How much time do I want to spend on networking, and when will I do it?
- How will I know when I've been successful?

Step one: Find out more about the ideas behind networking

The more self-effacing amongst us feel uncomfortable about the idea of networking. If you're one of those people, try to see the positive benefits of putting yourself 'out there'. For example, research has shown that people who have a good network of contacts, who are involved in professional and community activities outside the normal job, and who look for opportunities to be visible are more successful in their careers and contribute more effectively to the company they work for.

TOP TIP

Once you start to build your network, you'll find that it becomes a way of life and is something that you do all the time and instinctively. As you build professional relationships, be constantly thinking: 'What can I offer this person?', 'How can I be of help?'. The more you try to be of service to others, the more people will want to do things for you.

Step two: Be clear about the purpose of your networking

There are many reasons why you might want to network and market yourself. Our main focus here is looking for a promotion, but, if you're looking for a new job or even hoping to gain support for a major project, networking can help you too. Your efforts will be much more effective if you know exactly why you're building these relationships and what you hope to accomplish. Everyone has limited time, and this will help you to decide how to prioritise your networking activities.

Step three: Make a list of your strong points

It's important to have a sense of who you are and what your strengths are when you're networking and marketing yourself. Think about:

- your special skills and abilities
- any unique knowledge you have
- experiences that other people may find valuable
- characteristics and beliefs that define who you are

Knowing your strengths will give you a confidence boost and also help you to remember that other people will value what you have to offer.

TOP TIP

Never network from a position of weakness. Networking from a position of strength—and always having something of value to offer others—means that people won't see you as an annoyance. Also, try as far as you can to begin networking *before* you need anything from other people. People will be much more inclined to help you if you join or create a network to build relationships and do what you can to help others or the organisation.

Step four: Make a list of helpful organisations and events

Once you know your own overall goals and what you have to offer others, you can make a start on getting to know people who can help you.

First of all, find out about professional organisations and events that may be helpful to you in your career or with your project. Look for special interest groups, like those for 'entrepreneurial women', for example. Take the plunge and get involved!

When you're at professional events, like conferences, make sure that you attend social functions, that you join people for dinner, and that you seek out volunteer opportunities. Don't hide in your room and hope that people will come and seek you out.

If you're aiming to network within your current workplace, find out whether there are any special interest groups or social groups to join. If not, start some! Do a bit of 'market research' beforehand among your colleagues, and, if they're willing to come along, ask each of them to bring along someone else that the other attendees won't know—that will widen your pool of contacts. You could also look for committees to be involved in. Don't be shy about asking questions and making suggestions.

Step five: Create a contact list

Keeping in mind your reasons for networking, come up with a list of all the people you know who might be of help to you. Next, prioritise the list according to who is most likely to be helpful. Think about people you've done favours for in the past who might not be of direct help but who may know someone who can be. Once you've spoken to each person, ask him or her if they know of anyone else who might be able to help you. That way, your network grows larger at a stroke, and you have a personal recommendation to boot.

Step six: Create an action plan with a schedule

Take your list of organisations and events and your contact list, and put together an action plan for making connections. Schedule networking events in your diary, along with organisational meetings, conferences, and so on. If you're really determined, you could set up a timetable for making a certain number of calls per day or per week to the people on your contacts list.

Step seven: Meet up with people and attend events

It's now time to step out from behind the telephone or e-mail inbox! Meeting people and attending useful events is probably the best way of making the most of your network. Beforehand, review your list of strengths and focus again on why you're networking and marketing yourself in the first place. All of this will help you visualise a successful outcome, a very useful technique that can banish any last-minute nerves or self-doubt. Be friendly and professional, but most of all, be yourself.

TOP TIP

Always spend time connecting with people on a personal level *before* you ask for their help or share your reason for networking. If you're meeting in person with someone on your contact list, always bring a gift—something they can remember you by.

Networking on the Internet

While there's no substitute for meeting people face-to-face, it's not always possible. The Internet is a valuable place to make connections and to learn fruitful information from contacts all over the world. If you have a special interest or a special field, there is sure to be a newsgroup or threaded bulletin board on your topic.

Step eight: Market yourself

Marketing yourself goes hand-in-hand with building a network, and the two can complement each other powerfully. The strategy you use to market yourself will depend very much on your own personal goals but, as a general rule, think of yourself as a brand: 'Brand You'.

For example, when marketers are marketing a product, they look for the 'Unique Selling Proposition' (USP), something relevant and original that can be claimed for a particular product or service. The USP should be able to communicate 'Buy our brand and get this unique benefit'.

If you're marketing yourself, you need to use the same principles and define who your 'customers' are and what your USP is. Your list of strengths above should give you some clues, but the best USPs are short and snappy, such as 'I solve problems quickly and simply' or 'My leadership brings out the best in others'. The people closest to you can often give good suggestions if you get stuck.

Step nine: Keep an eye on your progress

It's always a good idea to keep track of your progress and of where you are in your action plan: a notebook or simple planner is all you need. It also helps to have someone as a sounding board, such as a friend, a family member, your boss, a mentor, or a professional adviser. When we feel accountable for our actions to someone we trust, we're much more likely to follow through. It's always a great boost to be able to celebrate your successes with someone else.

Step ten: Always say 'thank you'

As you build your network, many people will offer you information, opportunities, and valuable contacts. In your notebook, keep track of the favours that people have done for you and make sure that you write each one a short and simple thank-you letter or e-mail. People are always more willing to help someone who has been appreciative in the past.

Step eleven: Be patient!

Networking is a long-term activity. Steven Ginsburg of the *Washington Post* describes networking as 'building social capital'. You may not see results overnight, and at first should expect to give more than you get. But stick at it, because over time your network will become one of your most valued assets.

Common mistakes

✗ You don't want to bother anyone

Remember that people love to help others. Make sure, though, that you don't take up too much of someone's time and that you come well prepared. Be specific: say 'I'd like 30 minutes of your time', and then stick to it— don't outstay your welcome. Whenever you meet up with someone, always be thinking, 'Is there something I can do to help this person?' Create a win-win situation for everyone concerned.

✗ You come on too strong

Networking isn't about selling someone something they don't want. You're looking for opportunities to create a mutual relationship where there is give and take. For networking to be successful, you absolutely have to be interested in developing a long-term connection rather than grabbing a quick answer to a problem you're facing. Remind yourself that your focus is on relationship building, not on immediate results, and not exclusively on **you**.

✗ You don't come on strongly enough

If you put yourself in networking situations, but never talk about your needs or interests it may be that you're still not entirely sure why you've embarked on this route. Or maybe you've ended up networking for reasons that aren't as important to you as you thought they may be. If you're at all in doubt about what you want to achieve, go back to step one and clarify your purpose.

STEPS TO SUCCESS

✔ Understand that networking is an excellent way of building strong, long-term professional relationships that benefit everyone concerned, not just you.

✔ When you first think about networking, make sure you're absolutely clear about what you're hoping to achieve. Knowing your own goals is just as important as finding people to help you reach them.

✔ If you're naturally a shy person, you might feel uncomfortable at the prospect of putting yourself 'out there'. If you can see it as a key step towards reaching your career goals, though, it should become a much more attractive proposition.

✔ Make a list of your strengths to remind yourself of the skills, experience, and knowledge you have to offer others.

✔ Try to build your networks before you need to ask others for help. This will show that you're interested in building helpful alliances rather than just your own interests.

✔ Create a contacts list of all the people who might be able to help you, starting with those for whom you've done favours in the past.

✔ Put together an action plan of who you plan to contact when and which events might be useful to attend. Keep a track of your plan and your progress so that you can change tack if you need to.

✔ Think about how you can market yourself as well as network. Take a step back and see yourself as a 'brand' for a few minutes. All successful brands have

USPs, which set them apart from others. What is your USP?

✓ Never take advantage of other people's willingness to help you. If you say you'd like to book half an hour with someone to ask his or her opinion about something, stick to that time limit. Make a point of asking your contacts if you can help them.

✓ Always, always, thank people for their time and help.

Useful links

City Women's Network:
www.citywomen.org
Networking People UK:
www.npuk.com

Working with mentors

As we saw in chapter 6, building helpful relationships with others can give you a huge boost during your career and can come in especially useful when you're hoping for a move up the ladder. As well as building your wider network of contacts, you may also want to consider working with a mentor, either within or outside your current organisation. Mentors can be a great source of advice and encouragement, especially during fraught or tricky times at work.

Turning to your boss (or anyone else in your department, for that matter) for this kind of support is not always a safe or wise career move: let's say you and another colleague have both applied for the same promotion, clearly your boss cannot be seen to be helping one of you more than the other. You may not even have that great a relationship with your boss and you might be worried that this is blighting your promotion prospects. This is where mentors come into their own.

A mentor is someone who is committed to helping you find a path to success, helping you to gain the insight and contacts that you need in

order to understand the steps to your future. He or she should also be able to provide wise advice for your incidental crises and decision crossroads. Read on to find out if working with a mentor can help you get the career results you've been looking for.

Step one: Think through some common questions about mentoring

1 Can I trust my mentor to keep what we talk about confidential?

You should be able to. How else would you be able to learn, if you didn't have someone to ask all those questions you're too embarrassed to discuss with your boss? The ideal mentor relationship is based on trust and open communication. If you decide to work with a mentor, make it clear from the very outset that you'd like anything you say to him or her to remain between the two of you.

2 What if there is no-one at my company whose guidance I especially value?

Your mentor can come from anywhere: he or she could be a current or former colleague or even someone you've met at a special interest group or conference. In fact, you can have more than one mentor. It doesn't matter at all where they come from, as long as they're not your direct supervisors or in your department, and as long as they have the insight and experience that you value.

3 Do I have to pay for these services?

No. Most people are incredibly flattered to be asked to take on a mentoring role and see it as an honour. Those who have been high achievers in their own careers consider it good professional 'citizenship' to help those just starting out. It's natural that there will be some people less willing to help, of course, but try not to get downhearted: see it as reflection on them, not you.

4 Can I be a mentor, too?

Yes. Although you might not be that high up the career ladder to be someone immediately marked out as a mentor, any time you're willing to share advice and information to benefit someone else, you're fulfilling that role. Many organisations consider mentoring a valuable hallmark of leadership material. While you may be doing it out of kindness, others will take note and it will benefit your career in the long run.

Step two: Decide what you want out of a mentoring relationship

As with any scenario at work, you'll get much better results if you know exactly what you're hoping to gain. For example, are you:

- looking for guidance on building a career within one particular organisation?
- looking for help in developing your professional skills?
- looking for introductions into seemingly 'closed' circles of influential people?

The answers to these questions will help you decide whether you need a mentor within your company or elsewhere in your community or profession.

TOP TIP

Don't think that mentoring is a way of being spoon-fed useful information. The mentee has an important part to play in setting the agenda for the relationship and he or she also has to be in the right frame of mind to make it work.

Just as importantly, you have to think about whether you're the right type of person for this type of relationship. What could you bring to it? For example:

- Are you committed to contributing to the profession as well as developing your career?
- What will make the mentor glad to have invested time and energy in helping you along?
- Do you listen carefully to expert opinions and follow advice, or do you resist guidance?

TOP TIP
**Some people just aren't very good at taking
any feedback about their professional life,
even when it's meant constructively. Do be
honest with yourself, and, if you are one of
these people, having a mentor just might not
be for you. You may feel under attack, and the
mentor may become discouraged if their
advice is always batted back at them.**

Step three: Look for candidates

If you've decided that you would benefit from a mentoring
relationship, you now need to find the right person. Let
people know that you're on the look-out for a mentor
in a specific area of your life and ask for
recommendations.

Also, check whether there's an official mentoring
programme sponsored by your company and, if one does
exist, let the organiser know that you'd like to participate.
Eligibility for mentorship varies from one organisation to
another. If you're ineligible where you work, look for mentors
elsewhere. Spread your net wide and think creatively. You
could look for a mentor in your professional association,
community centre, local chamber of commerce or service
organisations, your college or university association, for
example.

Step four: Interview your candidates

It makes a lot of sense for you to whittle down your potential mentors into a shortlist and then find out the best candidate. Don't take the first one that comes along, just because you're keen to get things moving. The relationship you have with your mentor will be a working one, so you need to know that you're personally compatible and on the same wavelength.

Let the candidate interview you, too, without getting defensive or stressed. This is a low-pressure, getting-to-know-you step that, if done properly, will save a lot of time in the future.

TOP TIP
Remember that you can end a mentoring relationship at any time. It may be that, as your relationship progresses, you find that your views on life aren't as compatible as you'd thought. Don't feel as if you've failed: just move on and appreciate the progress you've made anyway.

Step five: Establish ground rules

Once you've picked your mentor, it's a good idea to work out the basic practicalities of your relationship. Once you've got these sorted out, you're both free to concentrate on the task in hand. For example, ask yourself:

- How often do you and the mentor want to meet?
- Does your mentor mind being called during the working day and/or at home?
- How often do the two of you want to review the relationship?
- How will you handle disagreements?
- If one of your goals is to meet people who could help you climb the career ladder, what will your mentor need to feel confident enough in you to start introducing you to his or her circles of influence?

Step six: Consider being a mentor yourself

Being a mentor is a rewarding way of building both your career and your profession in general. It can connect you with fresh ideas and ways of looking at the same old problems, and is an excellent way to network. As your mentees move on in their own careers, your network and sphere of influence expands as well.

Common mistakes

✗ You look to your boss to be your mentor

Avoiding that mistake is simple: just don't do it. If you've told your boss that you're hoping to work with a mentor, he or she may feel offended if you choose someone else, but explain diplomatically that it is common practice to look outside one's immediate circle at work to find a mentor. It means that there are no conflicts of interest.

✗ You became frustrated

In your initial conversations, make sure that you and your mentor share the same goals for your relationship. Also discuss your ideas of how quickly to expect projects to be done and what kind of reporting system will work for you. The clearer you both are about what is supposed to happen when, the less likely you are to have basic misunderstandings. Be prepared for things to go awry at times: not everything will work on the first attempt, but review your progress so far, and keep positive.

STEPS TO SUCCESS

✔ Understand what mentoring can offer you. It's an excellent way to benefit from someone else's experience.

✔ Mentoring is a relationship you have to work at. Don't expect it to lead to an automatic shoe-in to a top job.

✔ Your mentor doesn't have to come from within the company or organisation you're working for at the moment—in fact, it's probably better if he or she has some professional distance.

✔ Your boss could feasibly be your mentor, but someone not involved with the nitty-gritty of your everyday working life is much more likely to see better ways of working or new opportunities you may not have noticed.

✔ Mentoring relationships should be confidential and your mentor will understand that. However, it can't hurt to state this clearly before you start to meet.

✔ Mentoring is not something you pay for. If any of your potential mentors suggest that you should, politely decline and walk away.

✔ To get the best from this type of professional relationship, be very clear about what you're expecting to get from it. This will help 'frame' your meetings and help your mentor to understand your personal goals.

✔ Do make sure that you're the right type of person to enter into this type of relationship. If you find it hard to concede that others may have a fair point or to take constructive feedback positively, it could be that working with a mentor just isn't for you.

Useful links

Clutterbuck Associates:
www.clutterbuckassociates.co.uk
Institute of Leadership:
www.iofl.org

Succeeding as a new manager

Congratulations! Your promotion campaign has been successful and you're now a manager—either for the first time, or for the first time at this level. You're likely to be responsible for managing a team of up to 15 people, either in a company you already work for, or in a new organisation. This is obviously very exciting for you, though you may feel somewhat daunted at the prospect, especially if you were previously a member of the team you will now be managing.

However, provided you follow a few basic rules, there is no reason why such fears shouldn't be easily overcome, and your new role will give you excellent scope to stretch your wings and fulfil your potential. This chapter will give you these basic rules and help to smooth the path forward into this new phase of your working life.

Step one: Think about some key questions

1 I'm worried I might not be up to the job. How can I overcome my nerves?

It's only natural to have some feelings along these lines, and most people do when faced with a new challenge. Try to keep your worries under control, though, as a crisis of confidence may affect your chance of success. Keep positive and remind yourself of your skills and competence to do the job—after all, the company has recognised them, otherwise you wouldn't have been offered the role! Look after your health too: make sure you get plenty of sleep and exercise, so you feel fighting fit and ready to take on anything.

2 Is it likely that my new job will affect my home life?

Almost certainly, yes. Moving into any new job can be stressful, and even more so when new or extra levels of responsibility are involved. The trick is to make sure you're prepared for it and to face the fact that your life may be more demanding than ever before. Talk this over with your family and friends at an early stage; it will be a huge help if they are ready to lend their support while you get to grips with your new role, and also keep 'home' distractions to a minimum as you're settling in, so that you can focus.

3 Will I need to change my persona at work?

No, not essentially, but you may need to adjust your attitude
and the way you think about your job. A lot of management
is about standing back from the detail and seeing the 'big
picture' of what is happening so that you can make strategic
decisions about how to act. Rather than getting involved in
the nitty-gritty of individual tasks (as you may have done as a
team member), try to take an objective overview. If you can
learn to see the wood for the trees, you'll naturally behave in
a way that suits the circumstances.

Step two: Research and plan your new job

First things first: if you're moving to a new company to take
up your job, find out everything possible about it, the
department or section you'll be in, the job itself, and anything
else you can think of.

If you're moving up the ranks at your current place of work,
you'll know much of this already, but whatever the situation,
don't prejudge what you're going to find and don't be bound
by what you've done before or how any of your previous
employers operated.

From all this information, try to form at least a tentative
plan in advance—it's much harder to do this once you're
in the post. For example, what do you want to achieve?

How might you need to develop yourself to match the new demands? Think honestly about your strengths and weaknesses: how can you use your qualities and experience to their best advantage, and compensate for your limitations?

Step three: Engage with your team

Once you start your new job, make this your first priority. You need to know:

- the purpose of your department, team, or unit and its goals
- the work being done
- the current state of play
- any customer expectations that need to be met

Get all your team members together as soon as possible to introduce yourself, and then arrange meetings with each of them individually. Keep these meetings as friendly and informal as you can, but allow a generous amount of time and plan some kind of framework for the discussion. Listen carefully to what people have to say, and get information about them as individuals. Most importantly, ask each person the question: what should I do or not do to help you to perform your job effectively?

TOP TIP

Listening—and tuning in properly—to your team's concerns is a key part of your early days in a new job. That doesn't mean for a moment that you should promise them the moon, but simply that you'll be in a much better position to represent those concerns better to your own managers. You need to be able to fight your team's corner.

Step four: Plan some 'quick wins'

Next, plan a few targets that you can hit quickly and easily, all of which will help you to feel more at home and on top of things. Achieving these also eases the pressure you feel to perform and create a positive first impression, and begins the relationship-building process. Quick wins might include things like familiarising yourself with systems or ways of working if you're new to the company (for example, the internal e-mail system); setting up an early discussion with your line manager, arranging introductory meetings with suppliers or customers (external and internal), or even taking your team to the pub one lunchtime.

Step five: Clarify what expectations others have of you

You may be lucky enough to have been given a detailed job description, but the chances are there are still large gaps in your understanding of the task and priorities, what is or isn't acceptable in the new environment, and on what criteria you will be judged by your boss, peers, customers, and others. Don't be afraid to ask a lot of questions to clarify these issues, and then be very honest with yourself. Can you meet these standards? If not, what might you need to do, who could help, and what might the price be?

The perils of the 'new broom' syndrome

While you'll be keen to get going in your new role and make your mark, do tread carefully—at least to start with. Don't assume that your new team will welcome your style or your ideas with open arms, even if your predecessor was unpopular. They need to feel they can trust you and that you respect what they've been doing previously, before you can count on their support and co-operation.

Above all, don't depart too dramatically and quickly from established practice: even if you're desperate to change 'the way things are done around here', people are much less likely to throw their hands up in horror if you tackle things gradually. That doesn't mean that you do nothing, simply that you filter new ideas and ways of working bit by bit.

Step six: Show your commitment to individual development

From your initial meetings with your team, you will know what their individual aspirations and hopes are for their jobs going forward. Follow up by setting a code of management practice that you tell all team members about, and then follow it rigorously. This code might include commitments to assess training needs, to hold regular team meetings and one-to-one sessions, to set specific goals, and to evaluate performance against these goals.

Support this code by the way you yourself behave towards team members. Make a point of appreciating extra time and effort that people put in, listen properly to what they say, and be generous in your praise of their good qualities or achievements. The point is, by demonstrating to your team that you as their manager are on their side and will do everything in your power to support them, you will gain their trust and acceptance, and the performance of the whole team will be greatly enhanced.

Step seven: Lead by example

A good manager is also a role model, so it almost goes without saying that you must set an example for how you want your team members to behave. Lead by involving people in establishing group objectives, setting standards, and achieving deadlines, and demonstrate your own strong personal commitment to achieving the team's goals. Set an example too by maintaining high standards in your appearance and general behaviour, and by establishing warm, friendly relationships.

TOP TIP

In most workplaces, there's nearly always someone who is a nightmare to work with. Before you were a manager, if you had a troublesome colleague, you may have let off steam about him or her to a friend in the office. Being a boss doesn't mean you have to be a saint, clearly, but it does mean that you have to be extremely careful about what you say about colleagues and to whom. Even if you feel like screaming, don't commit any derogatory comments about a colleague to e-mail: it's all to easy to inadvertently send them to the wrong person. Also be careful about conversations you have in the office— you could be overheard. Use your common

---

**sense, and, if you can, wait until you get home
and unburden yourself to someone
completely outside of your work life: your
partner, friends, family members, or pet!**

Step eight: Take stock regularly

At end of your first week, identify issues that need attention
and make a plan for the following week. Get into the habit
each week of setting aside some time for review and
planning. Don't let your mistakes lead to self doubt:
everyone makes them. The key thing to remember is that
good managers learn from their mistakes, while bad ones
repeat them.

Common mistakes

✗ You make promises that may be difficult or impossible to keep

It is very tempting, during the phase of settling in and
relationship building, to make all kinds of promises to
your team, boss, or customers in the interests of creating
a good impression. Do remember, though, that you'll be
judged on whether or not those promises are fulfilled, so
be cautious about what you say you'll deliver. It's much
better to under promise and over deliver.

✗ You form alliances based on first impressions

Common myth has it that first impressions usually turn
out to be accurate, but this is often not true. Your

understanding of people and circumstances may change substantially as you learn more about them — especially if you've moved company and are grateful for a friendly face in your first few weeks — so don't cement yourself into new relationships that later turn out to be inappropriate or which might alienate other, potentially more useful, allies.

✗ You miss being friends with your team

This is probably the hardest part of promotion for many people: you're thrilled at the great opportunity you've earned, but know that your relationships with many people will change irrevocably. Whether you're new to just the job or the company, you need to build good relationships with your team members but also distance yourself a little from those who report to you so that you can be objective and unbiased in the way you work with them. This can be difficult when you have previously been a member of the team yourself, but, if you don't, you run the danger of being seen as a manager who has 'favourites' and of allowing your personal feelings to affect your judgment. This won't be good for your team's morale and you'll also lose much of your authority. It's probably best to be honest about how you feel with particular friends so that you are seen to maintain a professional relationship at work, and you can then keep purely social activities for outside the office.

✗ You're trapped into accepting the status quo

Whatever anyone says about 'the way things are done round here', the old ways are not always the best. Reserve your right to postpone judgment until you are thoroughly familiar with your team and your role, and then, if things need changing, change them, remembering to be sensitive in the way you do it.

STEPS TO SUCCESS

✔ Don't let worries about your new job get the better of you. Your skills and experience have got you this far, so keep positive and enjoy the challenge.

✔ If you're a 'details' person, you might find it hard to let go of some tasks so that you can concentrate on the bigger picture—the goals your team, department, and company need to meet. That's exactly what you must do, though, so be ready to adjust.

✔ Research and planning will help you to make a smooth transition into your new role. Find out exactly what's expected of you and come up with a basic plan of action.

✔ Spend time getting to know your team and listen carefully to what they have to say—they could prove to be your greatest allies.

✔ Don't over promise, though. It's tempting to get people

on-side by telling them exactly what they want to hear, but you'll end up backing yourself into a corner.

✔ Plan some quick wins to help you feel more in control.

✔ Tread carefully at first if you're introducing change. People's knee-jerk reaction to change tends to be negative, but, if you bring it in gradually, you'll get a less panicky response.

✔ Be very careful about what you say—and to whom—about your colleagues at work, even if they're driving you mad. Use your common sense and be discreet, however angry or upset you are.

✔ Don't beat yourself up if you make mistakes. Experience is the best teacher you'll ever have.

Useful links

HR Guide:
www.hr-guide.com
HR Next:
www.hrnext.com
HR Village:
www.hrvillage.com

Where to find more help

How to Get the Perfect Promotion: Your Guide to Career Progression
John Lees
Maidenhead: McGraw-Hill, 2003
224pp ISBN: 0077104269
Offering sage advice to job-hunters as well as those hoping to advance within their current organisation, this book offers practical and creative help on career advancement.

How to Be Brilliant
Michael Heppell
Harlow: Prentice Hall, 2003
224pp ISBN: 0273675826
Packed with techniques, strategies, and advice on how to make the most of your potential, this book is an excellent first step if you feel you need to turn your life around.

I Don't Know What I Want, But I Know It's Not This: A Step-by-step Guide to Finding Gratifying Work
Julie Jansen
London: Piatkus, 2004
270pp ISBN: 0273675826
A useful resource for anyone unhappy at work. Full of exercises to assess the reader's personality and skills, this book will help people to understand their present situation and come up with ways to find the job or career they really want to embark on.

The Ultimate Guide to Successful Networking
Carole Stone
London: Vermilion 2004
176pp ISBN: 0091900255
This book is a guide to communicating more effectively in all areas of life so that confidence increases and new contacts can be made. The author overcame her own childhood shyness to become a successful radio producer.